I0483011

TABLE OF CONTENTS

How to Get FREE Publicity and Interviews
Free is good but FREE does have a price!
©Copyright 2013 by Dr. Leland Benton

DISCLAIMER AND TERMS OF USE AGREEMENT:

(Please Read This Before Using This Book)

This information is for educational and informational purposes only. The content is not intended to be a substitute for any professional advice, diagnosis, or treatment.

The author and publisher of this book and the accompanying materials have used their best efforts in preparing this book.

The author and publisher make no representation or warranties with respect to the accuracy, applicability, fitness, or completeness of the contents of this book. The information contained in this book is strictly for educational purposes. Therefore, if you wish to apply ideas contained in this book, you are taking full responsibility for your actions.

The author and publisher disclaim any warranties (express or implied), merchantability, or fitness for any particular purpose. The author and publisher shall in no event be held liable to any party for any direct, indirect, punitive, special, incidental or other consequential damages arising directly or indirectly from any use of this material, which is provided "as is", and without warranties. As always, the advice of a competent legal, tax, accounting, medical or other professional should be sought where applicable.

The author and publisher do not warrant the performance, effectiveness or applicability of any sites listed or linked to in this book. All links are for information purposes only and are not warranted for content, accuracy or any other implied or explicit purpose. No part of this may be copied, or changed in any format, or used in any way other than what is outlined within this course under any circumstances. Violators will be prosecuted.

Introduction – The Power of Publicity

First, please allow me to dispel a myth: **Free is good but FREE does have a cost** and when it comes to Free Publicity, the cost includes the investment of your time and or offering free products/services.

Perseverance is need here because some sites will try your patience until you get to know their submission requirements.

A good many people make advertising and marketing difficult. It actually boils down to one simple factor, "The more ad impressions you place in the marketplace, the more sales you make!" Everything else is pure commentary.

Free publicity has its draw backs; for example you cannot be fussy and pick such things as demographics, ad location, time of run, etc. You take what you can get!

4

Is Free Publicity worth it? You betcha, but I just wanted to point out some of the downsides to using this amazing marketing tool.

Let's face it; in today's sluggish and recessionary economy, free is good. Whenever you can bring your economies-to-scale in line and maximize your marketing efforts at the same time then this is always good.

This book is the sequel to my best-seller book, "**Star Power - Using Celebrities for Interviews & Promotions**" http://www.amazon.com/dp/B00CJSWN6K.   It is my goal to provide my readers with all the tools they need to effectively market not only books but any product and service. This book is also a part of my ePublishing series of books:

*Copyright Law Guidebook
http://www.amazon.com/dpB00BHEYBK8
*Distraction Video Marketing
http://www.amazon.com/dp/B00BURDLAI
*How To Create, Market & Sell Audiobooks

http://www.amazon.com/dp/B00BQZXBZE

*How to Promote Your Book Online & Offline Vol 1

http://www.amazon.com/dp/B00AS7PDCK

*How To Promote Your Book Online & Offline Vol 2

http://www.amazon.com/dp/B00BDTEILO

*How To Promote Your Book Online & Offline Vol 3

http://www.amazon.com/dp/B00C42T2JC

*How to Write a Kindle Book in Hours

http://www.amazon.com/dp/B008XOY8VC

*How to Write Compelling Content

http://www.amazon.com/dp/B00B5QWYTI

*International Standard Book Numbers

http://www.amazon.com/dp/B00B2YB4SK

*Promoting Your Video Book Trailers

http://www.amazon.com/dp/B00BCDHEMG

*Publish with a Purpose

http://www.amazon.com/dp/B008Z5U4LC

*Star Power - Using Celebrities for Interviews & Promotions

http://www.amazon.com/dp/B00CJSWN6K

*The Overwhelmed Author

http://www.amazon.com/dp/B00CBI3XA8

*The ePubWealth Program

http://www.amazon.com/dp/B008HHHVO6

*The ePubWealth Program ADVANCED

http://www.amazon.com/dp/B00B65PGCA

*The Publishing Agreement

http://www.amazon.com/dp/B00BKGTQZI

*Viral Image Marketing

http://www.amazon.com/dp/B00C4MFGJ2

Taken all together, my ePublishing series of books is designed to educate authors on topics of interest that they should know.

Okay, now let's get to the good stuff…

Chapter 1 – How to Get Free Publicity

You would be stunned at how newspapers, magazines, radio and TV stations get their news stories? Surprisingly, the majority of the stories come from press releases sent by someone *promoting* their own cause or business? Yep, they come from YOU!

Media of all types need stories and you are the one that provides it.   You need publicity to promote your business so the relationship is symbiotic or mutual. It is quite possible to get your company mentioned on national television, major newspapers and magazines. AND, you may even be able to appear on TV talk shows, in front of millions of people. It is also possible to do countless interviews on the radio, right from your own home or office on the phone or Skype. All of the TV interviews I have given have been conducted using Skype. They rock too!

And guess what? It's all FREE! When you purchase advertising space in newspapers, magazines, on TV and radio, you can spend a small fortune, and have limited success.

With FREE publicity, you get exposure in a more credible, believable forum. And add to the mix the prestige that goes along with being labeled an expert.

I am, among other things, a forensic investigator and my company – ForensicsNation – and it has over 22,000 investigators all over the world.

I give interviews to sell my Cyber Crime/Cyber Forensics series of books:

Cyber Crime/Cyber Forensics

Confessions of a Child Predator
http://www.amazon.com/dp/B007BB97KU
Child Watch
http://www.amazon.com/dp/B0095K1P3M
Cyber-Daters Beware
http://www.amazon.com/dp/B006J9T4NA
Cyber Protect Your Business
http://www.amazon.com/dp/B0095JEAYY
ForensicsNation Bushwhacker Program
http://www.amazon.com/dp/B007I9AHVS
ForensicsNationsStore.com Catalog
http://ForensicsNationStore.com
Protecting Yourself from Cyber Crime
http://www.amazon.com/dp/B0095J3EIW
Stealing You
http://www.amazon.com/dp/B00778TT6E
Was Sandy Hook a Hoax?
http://www.amazon.com/dp/B00BFSM8IS
Why Women Should Not Use Online Dating Services

http://www.amazon.com/dp/B006J9EMH8
You Can Run But You Cannot Hide
http://www.amazon.com/dp/B006JLVZC6

I sell a good many books because of the "fear' factor people have with all the current news events scaring the living snot out of people.

Sex – humor – and fear sells anything!

One of the set sites to secure free interviews is HelpaReporter.com. In fact, most of the interviews I give come from this one site. It is free to join and the site sends out four emails/day listing interviews reporters are looking for. You respond directly to the reporter citing your credentials – education and career history, books written on the subject, products you offer to solve the problem, etc and the reporter will write back and schedule an interview if they like what you send them.

Here is an important fact about human behavior; when you read a story in the newspaper, you tend to believe it. When you see an advertisement for a product *right next to that newspaper article*, you tend to ignore it or not believe the ad, right? Of course! People believe stories in the media but discount advertising completely.

So how do you *get* this FREE publicity? How do you get *your* "believable story" in the media? I've put together several resources to help you get started.

Check out Internet News Bureau's http://www.internetnews.com/?8405 full array of publicity services if you don't have time or the inclination to do it yourself. They can write your press release, and then distribute them to a broad or a targeted list of journalists.

InternetSuccessStories.com

Finally, *here is* **free** publicity if you have a successful website! If you have experienced success on the Internet--any success at all--then you need to visit http://www.InternetSuccessStories.com and post YOUR success story. This site will become a high traffic site, offering stories from successful web site owners all over the world. Make sure you get *your* story posted right away. It's FREE!

Okay, later on in this book in Chapter 3, I will give you oodles of free publicity sites to choose from and make a splash in launching your product/service.

Remember to pace yourself and not become an "interview' hound. And do not be afraid to negotiate with the interviewer that you want your product/service/book mentioned in the interview too.

Now let's discuss how to get free interviews in more detail...

Chapter 2 – How to Get Free Interviews

Getting free interviews isn't a difficult task and one of the pitfalls is that you can easily become "trapped' devoting a good amount of time to giving interviews that take you away from your work. I once did 12-interviews in one day and I have never been so exhausted in my life.

Once you are labeled an "expert" in your field, the interview requests come flooding in so be careful and pace yourself.

Below I have included a couple of article I think you will find interesting. These should allow you to get an excellent handle on getting free interviews.

How to Get Interviewed on Podcasts for Free Radio Publicity

http://www.radioguestlist.com/how-to-get-interviewed-on-podcasts-for-free-radio-publicity.html

To get interviewed on podcasts as a "Guest Expert" is a great free publicity opportunity today. Similar to getting booked on radio programs or TV shows, you can get a lot of free publicity and attract attention to your products or your public relations clients by being interviewed on podcasts.

Many public relations professionals and marketing people are still unaware of the promotional power of podcasting. If you spend the time to reach out to podcast producers, talk show hosts, and the podcasting community, you can be rewarded with free guest expert interviews that attract new customers for your business from podcast listeners worldwide.

How to Be Interviewed as a Podcast Radio Guest Expert

Identify radio shows that book guest experts like you for interviews: The fastest way to do this is simply to search on Google using search terms like "podcast"+ "your topic". The iTunes podcast library is another good place to research podcasts that may want to interview you. You can also try podcast directories like PodcastDirectory.com, PodcastAlley.com, or Podbean.com to find shows interviewing guests like you (or your publicity clients).

Find the web site for the podcast to find contact info for the producers and bookers. For most Internet-only podcasts, the host also books the guests. The podcasts of larger "real" radio shows are usually just recordings of their broadcast radio program, so their guest interview booking is usually handled by their radio show producers instead of the host.

Create and send a pitch specific to that podcast. You need to e-mail, fax, FedEx, or call the producers to offer your expertise and information. Most podcasts are active in social media, too. So you can often reach them through Facebook, Twitter, or LinkedIn, if their contact info is not publicly available on their show web site.

Remember that Podcasters (or radio hosts or TV shows) are not interested in you or your products. Their goal is to find interesting new information that educates and/or entertains their audience. Your job is to craft a pitch that gets their attention by offering helpful details of your expertise that fit into their current radio show programming needs.

[Tip: Offer real information, not just a product pitch. A radio interview or TV segment is a big opportunity for you to establish yourself as an expert, not just to get a free commercial.]

While the strategies above are proven methods for getting interviewed on podcasts (and even getting booked to appear on TV), they are the same steps that thousands of other "guest experts" are following right now, too.

To get podcast interviews RadioGuestList.com is another solution.

If you're still wondering "how to get interviews", today you can skip many of the steps above by signing up for the free RadioGuestList.com podcast, radio and TV interview booking service.

This free podcast interview and TV public relations service will send you an e-mail each day with guest expert interview opportunities from real radio, TV, and podcast show producers who are looking for expert guests to interview "on the air".

Each RadioGuestList.com "Guest Request" email is a "live" booking opportunity submitted to RadioGuestList.com by a real show host or producer. The daily emails tell you exactly what type of guest interviews that radio show, TV producer or podcast host is looking for – all you have to do is reply by email to those that are seeking guest experts like you for their shows!

Visit http://www.RadioGuestList.com now to sign up for this free service. You'll start getting free radio and TV "guest requests" from podcasters by e-mail tomorrow!

Become a "Featured Guest Expert"

To make sure that radio producers, TV bookers, and podcast hosts worldwide are aware of your guest expert interview availability, you can also advertise on RadioGuestList.com as a "Featured Guest Expert".

As a "Featured Guest Expert" sponsor, RadioGuestList.com will feature your expertise, your photos, and any products that you want to promote on its popular website. Plus, Featured Guest Experts get their expert profiles e-mailed to its worldwide e-mail list of radio show hosts, TV bookers, and podcast hosts.

Becoming a "Featured Guest Expert" on RadioGuestList.com is a cost-effective and clever public relations strategy that can help raise your expert profile to get free radio, TV, and podcast publicity interviews.

More info: Sign up today at http://www.RadioGuestList.com to join the free radio, TV, and podcast guest interview booking service. Featured Guest Expert sponsorship information is available at http://bit.ly/ddLV6e

*****

How To Get Free Publicity For Your Business On TV And Radio

By Kerry McDuling January 17, 2011

Print media is just one avenue of publicity that is available. Depending on your business or story, radio, TV and online may be more appropriate. In this article, I share my top tips for attracting TV and radio coverage how to prepare for them.

TV And Radio Media

The main differences between broadcast and print are mainly quite obvious and determine the type of stories you pitch and the way you present them.

The same process as I discussed in my earlier article about print media applies.

Firstly determine your news story. Remember that, for TV, you will need a very visual story. If it's simply your point of view about your particular industry (eg, a comment about the property market if you are a real estate agent), this could still be applicable but you will need to find a visual angle to suggest to the reporter.

Broadcast news, both TV and radio, tends to be more instantaneous than print media, where you have both daily and weekly publications to pitch to. Therefore, ensure you get your news to the media outlets before it becomes old news, while it's still newsworthy. If your event happened yesterday or last week, there is not much

TV news can do with it, unless you find another follow-on angle.

Breakfast and magazine-style TV programs offer more flexibility in terms of news angles, and are not so focused on timeliness. However, because the stories tend to run for around 3 to 5 minutes, you will need to offer a lot more content than a simple news story.

Radio news is similar to TV news – bear in mind that, like TV news, you need to offer a spokesperson, usually yourself. If you are not prepared to speak to a journalist on TV or radio, and don't have anyone else appropriate that you can offer instead, broadcast may not be the right medium for you.

The best and most common way of communicating with the broadcast media is through preparing and distributing a **media release** to them. A media release is also known as a **press release** or a **news release**. As we have already looked at what goes into creating and preparing a media release, I won't repeat it here. But I would like to advise that for TV media, you should also include some ideas for visuals, and for both radio and TV, you should nominate your spokesperson on the document.

What Do You Do With Your Media Release?

The next thing to do is determine who you need to send your media release to. For radio news, find out a contact in the newsroom. If it's a radio or TV program, the program **Producer** is your contact. For TV news, it's the **Chief of Staff** or the appropriate reporter you need.

There are programs and services, such as *Media Monitors' Media Disk* and *Margaret Gee's Media Guide* in Australia with equivalents overseas, you can subscribe to that collect the names and contact details of all the journalists nation-wide. They cover television news and programs, radio programs, local, rural, community and metropolitan newspapers, national publications, industry publications and the glossy magazines you find in the news agency. There is an annual subscription fee to access these services year round.

Alternatively, if you already know what outlet you are targeting, you can simply find the phone number online, phone them and ask reception for the relevant person to send your media release to.

With TV and radio media, I always tend to follow up with a **phone call**. I would suggest you send the media release a couple of days before the event, or before you would like your story to go to air, and then follow up the morning before and then again the morning of the event.

For TV news, you often won't know until the last minute whether they will be able to have a crew available. For this reason, I would advise that you select a day that doesn't attract other big events or holidays. For example, one of my clients, a weight loss franchise, organized the hand-over of a car won by their "Slimmer of the Year"" on Remembrance Day. We didn't manage to get a TV crew out that day, because of all the Remembrance Day ceremonies that were taking place around the city, and therefore missed our opportunity with TV.

Tips For Broadcast Interviews

Radio interviews can usually be done over the phone, but on occasion, you may be called into a studio. Make sure you are in a quiet place without background noise where you won't be disturbed to take the call. Have your notes ready in front of you so that you don't panic and forget your message. Your 'umms' and 'ahhs' can be edited out if the interview is a recording, but best to try and keep them to a minimum if possible. For your first few, it may be a good idea to practice with family members and friends.

TV interviews can be especially daunting if you are new to them. Here are some tips that I give to my clients who are facing the exciting prospect of a TV interview.

- Reporters will often discuss in general what they're looking for prior to the interview, but they probably won't share the exact questions. A **spontaneous interview** will look and sound better.
- Once the interviewer starts, present your information in an organized way, keeping your answers brief! Remember that television is a medium comprised of sound and pictures. People view the images while listening to the sound and it's difficult for the listener to follow complex answers.
- When being interviewed, **listen carefully to the entire question** before answering. Have your facts straight and your numbers accurate.

- If you're not sure on what you want to say in response to a question, it's ok to pause for a moment and consider what you would like to say next.
- **Be conversational**. If you're discussing a complicated issue, pretend you're explaining it to your mother or to a child. Don't talk down to the viewers, but don't expect them to understand all the terminology.
- **Watch your gestures**. Don't let your head bob or your arms wave wildly, and if you are sitting down, don't swing on your chair. Try and stay still and composed. The camera will usually be on a tight "head shot" and you don't want to be moving in and out of frame.
- **Solid color clothing looks great on television**. Avoid patterns, especially small checks. They can cause the picture to shimmer which is very distracting. If you are outdoors, white is not a great idea and neither is black.
- Unless the circumstances are very special, **you will be responsible for your own hair and make-up**. Remember that under lights in a studio, you can look washed out and shiny, so don't be shy with a compact power that suits your coloring, even if you are a man, to get rid of any shine.
- Practice a smile and a considered look in the mirror. Obviously be genuine with your actions, but if your presentation is natural, and there are no awkward stand-out moments, everything else will flow.

Not everyone is a natural at radio or TV, but there is no denying that nothing beats the thrill of seeing yourself on TV or hearing your voice on the radio for the first time, and the time after that, and the time after that!

Good luck – you may even discover a hidden talent!

*****

Here is some good advice – practice speaking in a slow and articulate manner and be conscious of words you use that you constantly repeat. Record yourself speaking and you will be amazed at some of the habits you have acquired in speaking that are annoying and bothersome.

If you do a good job in an interview, the reporter will come back for more. Also develop a style. I was a standup comic for 10-years so I use quite a bit of humor in my speaking, which comes naturally to me but don't try humor if you aren't a natural comic.

Next, develop a response letter that lists all of the items I cite in Chapter 1 - education and career history, books written on the subject, products you offer to solve the problem, etc and have it available to send to any reporter. Spend some time with this letter and make sure there are no typos or errors and also make sure everything you cite is truthful and accurate.

Chapter 3 – How to Find Free Blog Comment Sites & Free Publicity Sites

In this chapter, I am going to load you up with free publicity sites where you can easily access all of the free publicity your heart desires. I have personally used a good many of these site (but not all of them0 and some are easy and some are difficult but you will soon develop a good understanding of what sites work best for your situation. So let's get at it, shall we/

http://www.9to5blogger.com/dofollow-blog-commenting-sites-list/400/

If you're a regular reader of 9to5Blogger, you might've noticed the improvement in page rank and monthly traffic. I mainly follow two **link building techniques to get quality backlinks** to my blog. This includes guest posting and do-follow blog commenting. One can get quality dofollow backlinks through these techniques and get rid of Google Algo Penalties.

And now, let's discuss about the in and out's of blog commenting.

Blog Commenting Guidelines

Blog commenting is undoubtedly one of the best sources of getting one way links pointing back to your website. Not just a backlink, you can even get traffic through commenting, but that too only when your comment is interesting.

- Mainly comment on blogs with relevant niche such as yours. This will add more weightage as you get links from relevant sites.
- Read before you take action: First read the entire article and the available comments, and then you can add some additional information regarding the topic or simply ask a question if you don't agree with the author's point.
- No one likes to see comments such as "superb blog", "thanks for sharing" or "see my blog" on their blog and so never ever comment without adding any value to the topic.
- Most of the blogs don't accept keywords as name and hence try to use *"Your real name @ keyword"* in the name field. If you find any blogs that accept keywords, then it is sure your luck. Go ahead and submit your comment with your targeted keyword in the name field. This will boost your rankings for sure.

There are actually two kinds of blog commenting techniques.

1. **DoFollow Blog Commenting**: This is the most widely used commenting technique. There are some blogs (listed below) which have a dofollow enabled commenting system. Commenting on such blogs will add some PR juice to your blog + some traffic if it is interesting.

   Disadvantage: You'll have less chances of getting huge traffic to your site using this technique due to the number of users commenting on dofollow blogs for PR.

2. **NoFollow Blog Commenting**: This is less widely used blog commenting technique. Make a note of some popular blogs in your niche and add useful comments on their blogs (especially on their popular posts and recent posts). Doing so, you'll get good number visitors from your comments on their blogs.

Disadvantage: Unlike dofollow blogs, you'll only get traffic and not any PR juice.

So, depending upon your need, you can follow whatever blog commenting technique suits you. But I personally suggest participating in both the techniques so that you'll get both traffic and some page rank.

How to Find Blogs in your Niche?

If you wanted to find the dofollow blogs in your niche manually, then please follow the below procedure.

- Perform a Google search of your niche
- Join any bloggers community like IndiBlogger or Bloggers.Com and you can easily find blogs based on your interested categories.
- Simply, use the free software called "Comment Kahuna".

In case you don't have enough time to find blogs to comment, below is a list prepared by us.

High Page Rank DoFollow Blogs List

DoFollow Blogs	Page Rank
http://weblogtoolscollection.com	6
http://www.seomoz.org/blog	6
http://comluv.com	5
http://www.bloggingtips.com	5
http://www.bluehatseo.com	5
http://seobythesea.com	5
http://freebloghelp.com	4
http://www.blogussion.com	5
http://kikolani.com	5
http://engineering.curiouscatblog.net/	5
http://www.quicksprout.com/	6
http://www.basicblogtips.com	5
http://www.comptalks.com	5
http://www.animhut.com/	5
http://blog.ruski.co.za/	5
http://newcritics.com	5

http://www.dumblittleman.com	5
http://www.currybet.net	6
http://www.bloggodown.com	4
http://www.blogengage.com	4
http://www.smartbloggerz.com	3
http://www.blogtap.net	4
http://www.webuildyourblog.com	4
http://www.weblogbetter.com	4
http://crayonwriter.com	4
http://dereksemmler.com/	4
http://www.articlesnatch.com/blog/	4
http://www.kongtechnology.com	5
http://www.trafficgenerationcafe.com	4
http://blog.2createawebsite.com	4
http://www.iblogzone.com	4
http://letsbuildwebsites.com	4
http://growmap.com	5
http://www.intenseblog.com	5
http://freakify.com	4
http://contentmarketingup.com	4
http://ariherzog.com	4
http://www.dreamsystemsmedia.com	4
http://wordpress-websitebuilder.com	4
http://www.jonathanvolk.com	4
http://blondish.net	4
http://www.wordsellinc.com	4
http://theadventurouswriter.com	4
http://www.tekkaus.com	3
http://www.windowstalk.org	4
http://www.howtospoter.com	4
http://www.benspark.com	4

http://www.famousbloggers.net	4
http://www.theemotionmachine.com	4
http://zebida.com	4
http://www.mariareyesmcdavis.com	4
http://forthelose.org	5
http://www.ewriting.pamil-visions.com	4
http://www.myrecycledbags.com	4
http://www.lauraroeder.com	4
http://www.kimwoodbridge.com	4
http://stopdropandblog.com	4
http://ariwriter.com/	4
http://blondish.net/	4
http://communicatevalue.com/	4
http://fatfightertv.com/	4
http://theadventurouswriter.com/	4
http://thesisthemehq.com/	3
http://www.barbaraling.com/	4
http://www.entrepremusings.com/	4
http://www.heartofbusiness.com/	4
http://www.howtospoter.com/	4
http://www.onewomanmarketing.com/	4
http://www.replaceyoursalary.com/	4
http://www.rockyourday.com/	4
http://www.sitesketch101.com/	4
http://www.smartbloggerz.com/	3
http://www.tekkaus.com/	3
http://www.webuildyourblog.com/	4
http://www.wordsellinc.com/	4
http://www.thevirtualhandshake.com/blog/	4
http://blogchef.net/	4
http://www.deardrmoz.com/	4

http://www.jhsiess.com/	4
http://www.uppergreenside.org/blog/	4
http://www.memwg.com/	4
http://www.steverenner.com/	4
http://www.articlesnatch.com/blog	4
http://www.communityspark.com	4
http://www.memwg.com	4
http://dmiracle.com	4
http://blog.atyq.info/	4
http://www.ruhanirabin.com	3
http://dofollow.info	4
http://www.theblog.ca	4
http://www.graphicdesignblog.co.uk	4
http://www.thevirtualasst.com/	4
http://www.techatlast.com	4
http://technoupdates.org/	3
http://superbloggingtips.com	3
http://emoneymarketing.com	3
http://www.bloggingjunction.com	3
http://www.seotops.com	3
http://www.extremejohn.com	3
http://win-with-1.com	3
http://another-blogger.com	2
http://seoaddicted.com	3
http://betterbloggingforbloggers.com	3
http://bloggingwithoutablog.com	3
http://www.geekblogger.org	2
http://wassupblog.com	3
http://www.blogstash.com	3
http://tycoonblogger.com	2
http://www.youdofollow.com	3

http://growwithstacy.com	3
http://shalusharma.com	3
http://www.techtricksworld.com	4
http://www.johncow.com/	3
http://www.pqinternet.com/	3
http://www.howtowakeupearly.com/	3
http://emoneymarketing.com/	3
http://pixelheadonline.com/blog/	3
http://revellian.com/	3
http://thereasoner.com/	3
http://superbloggingtips.com/	3
http://www.probloggingsuccess.com	3
http://www.blogengage.com/blogger/	3
http://www.3arn.net	3
http://www.itechcode.com	3
http://www.webmaster-success.com	3
http://www.thebadblogger.com	4
http://myblog2day.com	3
http://www.monetizeblogging.com	3
http://www.rsatechnologies.in	3
http://www.hacktabs.com	2
http://azblogtips.com	2
http://www.netchunks.com	3
http://getbusylivingblog.com	3
http://www.seommotips.com	3
http://www.blogelina.com	3
http://www.awesomebloggers.com	2
http://www.techblaster.net	3
http://www.magnet4marketing.net	3
http://www.blognetworking101.com	3
http://hotblogtips.com	3

http://www.labofweb.com	3
http://www.7boats.com	3
http://e-businessmoms.com/blog/	3
http://allbloggingtips.com	3
http://techjay.com	3
http://jamesmartell.com	3
http://www.waynejohn.com	3
http://www.fridaytrafficreport.com	3
http://wpbloghost.com	2
http://www.serradinho.com	3
http://www.juliesjournal.com	3
http://jamesmartell.com/	3
http://techiezlounge.com/	3
http://wassupblog.com/	3
http://www.fridaytrafficreport.com/	3
http://www.getpaidtowriteonline.com/	3
http://www.purposive.com/	3
http://www.waynejohn.com/	3
http://www.layercake.net/	3
http://blog.dmbcllc.com/	3
http://www.missnexus.com/	3
http://www.joebartender.com/	3
http://niceblogger.com	3
http://pixelheadonline.com/blog	3
http://www.howtowakeupearly.com	3
http://www.peterleehc.com/blog	3
http://tucsonseosolutions.com	3
http://www.tlmarketing.net	3
http://www.affiliatebestprograms.com	3
http://techpatio.com	3
http://followlist.com	3

http://annanta.com	3
http://www.serradinho.com/	3
http://www.9to5blogger.com/	2
http://bloggingfor.info	1
http://www.besttipsforblogging.com	2
http://ez-onlinemoney.com	2
http://www.dollarsblog.com	2
http://theblogabouteverything.com	0
http://blog.newmediabloggers.com	2
http://www.blogging-techies.com	2
http://www.bloggingwp.com	2
http://www.dollarsperday.net	2
http://www.interviewquestionshq.com	2
http://www.empressofdrac.com/	2
http://www.chatbugkaren.com/	2
http://hterry.com/	2
http://letssermo.com/	2
http://findmyblogway.com	2
http://oddblogger.com	3
http://www.ehowportal.com	2
http://www.howtomakemoneyonlineideas.com	2
http://www.maxblogtips.com	2
http://www.bloggingcage.com	2
http://www.techotalk.com	2
http://www.seoallrounder.com	2
http://www.blogging24h.com	2
http://www.geekrevealed.com	2
http://www.bloggersmakemoney.com	2
http://useme4info.com	2
http://www.johnbanksblog.com	2
http://rumahabi.com	2

http://www.marketingblagger.com	2
http://www.inlineseo.com	2
http://techshali.com	2
http://www.worthytips.com/	2
http://www.powerdosh.com	2
http://cashtactics.net	2
http://www.reviewerofsites.com	1
http://infodotnet.blogspot.com	2
http://www.yimto.com	2
http://www.learnblogtips.com	2
http://kathyblogger.com	1
http://www.adsenseurdu.com	2
http://www.daddydewberry.com	1
http://www.techehow.com	1
http://www.wpcypher.com	1
http://tagskitchen.com/	1
http://www.londonerlife.com/	2
http://www.betterbloggingways.com	2
http://moneyctl.com	2
http://www.teckilla.com	1
http://www.makemenoise.com	1
http://www.crunchyhub.com	1
http://www.guideandnews.com	1
http://www.saifullahbutt.com	1
http://blogpunch.com	1
http://techforwards.com	2
http://www.skillcollector.com	2
http://www.voice-broadcast.com	1
http://sighnetdollars.blogspot.com	1
http://tricksexpert.com	1
http://www.beginnerstip.com	0

http://www.source-blogger.com	0
http://www.affiliateblogonline.com	0
http://readmeloud.com	1
http://hitechzilla.com	0
http://techteen.net	4

Consider the following websites in which to submit your company to, and gain free publicity.

StartupWizz http://www.startupwizz.com/submit-a-startup/ was founded in 2009 as a place for entrepreneurs and investors to stay informed about startups on the web. The goal of startupwizz is to find some of the most disruptive, niche and interesting startups that their peers and investors want to know about.

GreatStartups http://greatstartups.com/submit-site/ writes about startups entering the market with growth potential or startups that have already been keyed as success stories. They also will cover startups that may be having problems or simply did not succeed due to various reasons. They note that some of the startups written about are not necessarily "great;" however, they do posses a quality that may be appealing to various readers.

KillerStartups.com http://www.killerstartups.com/ is a user driven internet startups community. Entrepreneurs, investors, and bloggers stay informed on up-and-coming internet startups using this blog platform, where internet entrepreneurs submit their startup to see what others think about it.

StartupWorld.com http://startupworld.com/ is dedicated to helping start-ups and developing businesses market their product or service. By joining StartupWorld.com you will be able to list your business for free.

StartupBooster.com
http://www.startupbooster.com/submit-site/ is a blog that helps online startups navigate through emerging technologies and marketing opportunities to succeed.

ExecutivePlan
http://www.businessplanexecutivesummary.com/ not only reviews new startup businesses on its widely read blog, it also aims to help entrepreneurs raise startup capital. They offer a number of free guides, articles, and videos on how to write an executive summary to raise capital from angel investors and venture capitalists

Squidoo: Submit   your   startup
http://www.squidoo.com/sumbit-startup website link on this simple website. Allows you to simply submit a link to your website with a 2 sentence description instead of a long application process. Then each week one startup will be chosen and featured on a widely read blog. Simply put, entrepreneurs need free publicity to get the word out about their startup company. Make sure to utilize all 7 of these resources to generate major buzz around your company without spending a dime.

Social Media - Facebook, Twitter, Google+ and LinkedIn; due to Google's reliance on their own pages for search engine results, having a Google+ page is essential if you want to be found locally."

Blogs - Contacting bloggers directly to ask for a pitch is a great way to get free publicity. Some businesses have had success doing this by offering a free product in exchange for the blogger hosting a giveaway. The business can give one free item to the winner of the giveaway, and then offer a discount to anyone else who follows that blog.

Nibletz: http://nibletz.com/ is a blog that allows you to pitch for the possibility of publication. "What makes them a great opportunity is that they publish a ton, which means you have a strong likelihood of being covered.

The Startup Pitch: http://thestartuppitch.com/, which invites every startup to pitch to the world at large.

Free Press Release Submission Sites

Pitch Engine: http://www.pitchengine.com/
PRLog: http://www.prlog.org/

LAST UPDATED ON SEPTEMBER 2012

UPDATED PRESS RELEASE LIST	PAGE RANK	GOOGLE WEBMASTER INDEXED PR	PAGE RANK
http://www.directionsmag.com	6	http://www.i-newswire.com	6
http://www.tmcnet.com	6	http://www.prlog.org	6
http://www.24-	6	http://www.information-	5

37

UPDATED PRESS RELEASE LIST	PAGE RANK	GOOGLE WEBMASTER INDEXED PR	PAGE RANK
7pressrelease.com		online.com	
http://www.news.thomasnet.com	6	http://www.ideamarketers.com	4
http://www.free-press-release.com	5	http://www.articlecirculation.com	4
http://www.openpr.com	5	http://www.free-news-release.com	4
http://www.promotionworld.com	5	http://www.1888pressrelease.com	4
http://www.downloadjunction.com	5	http://www.onlineprnews.com	4
http://www.indiaprwire.com	5	http://www.seenation.com	4
http://www.cgidir.com	5	http://www.pressreleasepoint.com	4
http://www.pressbox.com	4	http://www.prfocus.com	3
http://www.ecommwire.com	4	http://www.prhwy.com	3
http://www.pressbox.co.uk	4	http://www.prbd.net	2
http://www.freepressindex.com	4	http://www.freepressbox.com	2
http://www.newdesignworld.com	4	http://www.prtake.com	1
http://www.bignews.b	4	http://www.pralley.com	1

UPDATED PRESS RELEASE LIST	PAGE RANK	GOOGLE WEBMASTER INDEXED PR	PAGE RANK
iz			
http://www.addpr.com	4	http://www.prmarker.com	1
http://www.audiodirectory.nl	4	http://www.prcarrier.com	1
http://www.sanepr.com	4	http://www.adsrack.com	1
http://www.prurgent.com	4	http://www.multipressrelease.com	0
http://www.newsreleaser.com	3	http://www.pressreleaselogin.com	0
http://www.prsync.com	3	http://www.pressreleasebuster.com	0
http://www.exactrelease.com	3	http://www.pressreleasepack.com	0
http://www.newpressrelease.com	3	http://www.pressreleasebay.com	0
http://www.pressmethod.com	3	http://www.publishpressreleasenews.com	0
http://www.prurgent.com	3	http://www.pressreleasecomet.com	0
http://www.upvery.com	3	http://www.blinkpressrelease.com	0
http://www.freepressreleases.co.uk	3	http://www.guidepressrelease.com	0
http://www.express-	3	http://www.pressexposu	0

UPDATED PRESS RELEASE LIST	PAGE RANK	GOOGLE WEBMASTER INDEXED PR	PAGE RANK
press-release.net		re.com	
http://www.pressabout.com	3		
http://www.free-press-releas e-center.info	3		
http://www.itbsoftware.com	3		
http://www.pr4links.com	3		
http://www.pr9.net	3		
http://www.afly.com	3		
http://www.epicpr.com	2		
http://www.postafreepressrelease.com	2		
http:/www.yourfreepressrelease.net	2		
http://www.press-network.com	2		
http://www.netforcepress.com	2		
http://www.pressrelize.com	2		
http://www.pressreleaseset.com	2		
http://www.way2press	2		

UPDATED PRESS RELEASE LIST	PAGE RANK	GOOGLE WEBMASTER INDEXED PR	PAGE RANK
release.com			
http://www.jkhanok.com	2		
http://www.pressreleasepedia.com	2		
http://www.update.press-network.com	1		
http://www.top-best-news.com	1		
http://www.articlesubmission.org	1		
http://www.pr-usa.net	1		
http://www.pressreleaseleap.com	1		
http://www.free-pressrelease.org	0		
http://www.pressreleaseway.com	0		
http://www.pressreleasevisual.com	0		
http://www.pressreleasevision.com	0		
http://www.pressreleaseultra.com	0		
http://www.pressreleasetycoon.com	0		

UPDATED PRESS RELEASE LIST	PAGE RANK	GOOGLE WEBMASTER INDEXED PR	PAGE RANK
http://www.pressrelease4all.com	0		
http://www.pressreleasesplash.com	0		
http://www.freepressrelease.com	0		
http://www.pagerelease.com	0		
http://www.anyrelease.com	0		
http://www.pressreleasetwist.com	0		
http://www.pressreleasetime.com	0		
http://www.pressreleasethis.com	0		
http://www.pressreleasetalk.com	0		
http://www.pressreleasestatus.com	0		
http://www.pressreleasesection.com	0		
http://www.ratepressrelease.com	0		
http://www.pressreleasewheel.com	0		

UPDATED PRESS RELEASE LIST	PAGE RANK	GOOGLE WEBMASTER INDEXED PR	PAGE RANK
http://www.exactrelease.com	0		
http://www.newsinsites.com	0		
http://www.cliprelease.com	0		
http://www.clickanews.com	0		

Journalist Source Sites

Help a Reporter Out (HARO) http://www.helpareporter.com/
Reporter Connection http://www.reporterconnection.com/
Source Bottle http://www.sourcebottle.com/

Radio and Podcasts

RadioGuestList.com http://www.radioguestlist.com/

Chapter 4 – How to Get Free TV Ads

Here is a site that has a pretty good offer. Check it out: http://www.barenakedads.com/

Here is another site worth looking at: http://www.cheaptvspots.com/

TV ads are not completely free but almost. I have included a really good article in this section how to buy TV advertising on a budget...

http://www.inc.com/guides/2010/09/how-to-buy-tv-advertising-on-a-budget.html

How to Buy TV Advertising on a Budget

For small businesses, here's the reality of TV -- the medium can be an affordable messenger.

Television advertising is often bypassed by small and mid-sized businesses in favor of print, radio, and even Internet. They often view TV as too expensive and may believe that only large national companies can advertise on it. While that may have been true a generation ago, the advent of cable television and the explosion in the number of stations and programming has made TV an advertising medium that is effective for even local businesses -- a medium that businesses of virtually any size can afford.

"If you're a local firm, such as a jeweler, you don't need to run ads nationally," says J. T. Hroncich, managing director and principal of Capitol Media Solutions, an agency that helps companies buy advertising. "Cable TV is very reasonable. As opposed to taking out an ad during American Idol on broadcast TV, you can take out a local ad on a popular cable show, such as Top Chef. It all depends on who your target market is."

The following article will review why TV is a good advertising medium, how to target your TV ads, and how to buy TV advertising on a budget.

How to Buy TV Advertising on a Budget: Why Buy TV Advertising

For certain types of small or mid-sized businesses, television may be a better advertising medium than any other. "Television is an attractive use of an advertising budget since it maximizes the reach of a commercial message and provides the opportunity for your potential customers to visually understands your service or product," says Lori Weston, a freelance media professional working in the Boston market with media buying service, Media Period, of West Bloomfield, Michigan.

If your product is visually appealing -- such as an automobile or a Snuggie or diamond jewelry -- TV advertising may showcase that product better than other media, such as radio. "If you feel your product is better suited to people seeing it as opposed to hearing about it, then TV makes a lot of sense," Hroncich says.

What's more, television is "sexy," Weston says. "Television is captivating and holds an audience's attention," she says. "Additionally, if your ad fits in well with the programming where it's advertised, it could prove to be an outstanding tool in your marketing efforts."

Typically, an effective advertising campaign that includes TV advertising is expensive and complicated; however it does not always need to be. With some patience, good negotiating skills, and an open mind you can buy TV on a budget.

How Much a TV Ad Will Cost

Before jumping in, you need to understand your budget for advertising. Be sure to include the costs associated with producing your commercial. You can produce your ad independently or with a television station, but costs can vary wildly. "It really depends on what you want," Hroncich says. "If you're a family-run business and you want to film a 30-second spot that shows a screen shot of your dinner special, it's not going to be very costly. But if there are actors employed, that will cost you more." He estimates that TV commercials can cost anywhere from $2,500 and up.

Then there is the cost of the advertising campaign. You typically don't want to spend your advertising budget all at once. You want to air it with a bit of frequency so that people will see it a number of times and it reaches a larger percentage of your target market. Typically, television stations will accept spot lengths of 10, 15, 30, and 60 seconds, and even longer if it is a direct response ad, Weston says.

You may have access to co-op advertising funds from manufacturers of products you sell that would augment your budget, Weston adds. "If so, make sure that you clearly understand the terms of qualifying for those funds, for example the ad may need to run a specific number of times or within a definitive time frame," she says.

How to Buy TV Advertising on a Budget: Target Your TV Ad Campaign

Before launching a TV ad campaign, you need to develop a plan for who you want to reach where, when, and how. Here are some considerations.

Geography - Options for advertising on TV include national networks, which reach a national audience; local broadcast or independent stations, which reach a regional or local market; and cable television, which can be national, regional, or local. "Any one or a combination of these can be used to achieve success," Weston says.

Target audience - Who is your core customer? "If you are trying to sell hearing aids your target audience would likely be adults 55 and older," Weston says. "Do not, under any circumstance, believe everyone is in your potential market."

Timing and seasonality - Identify any days or seasons that have the greatest potential for increased revenue, i.e. furniture stores target weekends and ski retailers target winter, Weston says. Something to keep in mind is that rates change every quarter -- broadcast TV rates usually rise in the fall when the new season starts for certain shows. Also, when a hotly contested election is on the horizon, demand for TV spots in certain markets may rise, Hroncich says.

How to Buy TV Ads on a Budget

Now that you know the basics, here are tips on how to find the bargains when it comes to advertising on TV.

- **Pay upfront.** "Station sales representatives love this," Weston says. "They know the money is there, and their commissions are secured. They will work hard for you and maintain a schedule with little preemptions."

- **Commit to a multiple-week schedule.** Most cost-efficient packages are sold on a 10-13 week basis, Weston says. "Stations much prefer to have spots booked ahead of time," she adds. "It helps them manage their inventory." If you work through a cable company that has many different stations, you might be able to strike up multiple week deals on a variety of programs. "If you are looking to advertise during the weekend, you could strike up a 13-week weekend schedule whereby your ad runs in live sports programming and news, along with old movies and syndicated programs," Weston says.

- **Take advantage of market conditions.** If the local economy is slowing, chances are the airtime available on local television stations is aplenty and you can negotiate some terrific deals. That was the case during the recent economic downturn, when TV and cable companies were looking to fill their advertising slots and willing to negotiate.

- **Look for fire sales.** "Although they don't happen very often, fire sales provide the opportunity to purchase advertising packages far in advance," Weston says. Quite often, they will include programming you would otherwise not be able to afford.

- **Auctions.** When you purchase advertising via an auction, you will need to pay upfront, and may not have a clear understanding of what time slots you'll be receiving. Rather than base your entire television schedule on auctions, you may want to simply use the auction to complement your original schedule, Weston advises.

- **Buy remnant advertising.** You can purchase inexpensive remnant packages with a range of flexibility; the more flexible you are, the more savings you will receive. "For example, you can purchase an 'auto-fill schedule' of 100 spots per week to air 6 a.m.-12 a.m., Monday through Friday," Weston says. "It may seem like a risky schedule, however at such a low cost if one or two spots air in a popular program this essentially 'pays' for the remaining spots."

- **Negotiate added value.** When booking airtime, you can almost always negotiate for extras or "a value add," Hroncich says. "We did a cable TV buy for one of our clients recently and we got some free advertising on their website as a value added and some public service announcements at no charge." PSAs are 10-second spots to air when available during your flight (the schedule of advertising for a period of time). Hroncich says that advertising agencies can often help negotiate these value add deals better because they're aware of what the stations have offered other advertisers in the past.

- **Negotiate a media mix.** Ask if the television station has a website and see if there are any potential promotional activities on that website if you buy TV advertising. "Negotiate to have your video commercial stream on a website," Weston says. "This is where TV trumps radio." While still advantageous, a radio ad streaming online does not carry the weight of a TV ad.

As you fine tune your TV advertising schedules, you'll start to realize the two or possibly three stations that provide the most value, Weston says. "If it is completely obvious, it's okay to drop the other stations considered," she says. "Develop a relationship with your best performers and invest in them. It will be worth your effort."

*****

The article cites some very important points and gives some very salient advice. Buying TV ads cheaply is easy and with so many cable channels begging for advertising, they actually giveaway the show.

I watch the Military Channel on cable TV. They have about a dozen ads that they keep repeating over and over again and if this is annoying then I don't know what is.

And it is the same with most cable channels too! There are too many channels and not enough advertisers. Take advantage of this fact and get in while the going is good.

Chapter 5 – Where to Find a Good Publicist

A good publicist is worth their weight in gold and candidly they are not that expensive either.

I have provided an article below to help you understand what publicists do. The only part of the article that I disagree with is the part where it states that "Publicists are public relations professionals who represent celebrities rather than companies." This simply is not true. I have used a publicist for years and I m not famous.

How Publicists Work
By Dave Roos

http://www.howstuffworks.com/publicist.htm

Publicists are public relations professionals who represent celebrities rather than companies. It's hard to be famous. In the era of the 24-hour news cycle, there's no end to the public's hunger for the latest, craziest news, especially if it involves a celebrity. Young Hollywood actors are trailed by packs of roving paparazzi, and the pages of tabloid magazines are devoted to celebrities dressing badly, saying stupid things and being caught with people other than their spouse.

This is why actors, politicians, musicians, authors and other well-known public figures hire publicists. Publicists are public relations professionals who specialize in representing individuals rather than companies and large organizations. The job of the publicist is to manage the client's image in the eyes of the public. They do this by getting good press for their client in magazines, newspapers, TV shows and Web sites.

A good publicist knows all of the editors, journalists and TV reporters that work her client's beat. She knows how to pitch a story that writes its own headline. And she knows how to spin a possible publicity crisis into a golden opportunity. After all, "all publicity is good publicity."

What do publicists do? How do you succeed as a publicist? And, how do you break into the business?

Job Description of a Publicist

The main responsibility of a publicist is to get positive press coverage for his client. To do this, the publicist needs to create and maintain good relationships with journalists by sending them original, insightful, timely story ideas that involve the client in some way.

There are several different ways to **pitch** story ideas to journalists. Press releases are an easy way to send the same story pitch to multiple members of the media. The standard press release is written like a news story, complete with an attention-catching headline, a lead paragraph that hooks in the reader and quotes from sources. In the age of the fax machine and email, press releases are often lost in the overwhelming pile of junk that is sent to journalists on a daily basis.

A more effective way to get story ideas to a journalist is to cultivate a genuine, working relationship with reporters, editors and TV news producers. This means that publicists spend a considerable amount of time networking with members of the media. Much of their day is spent on the phone or firing off e-mails. Publicists work long hours and are expected to be available for the client day or night. After office hours, they attend parties and media get-togethers in the hope of getting face time with influential journalists.

The journalist/publicist relationship is a two-way street. What happens if the client does or says something incredibly stupid? Now it's the publicist who's receiving all of the phone calls and emails. If the publicist wants to maintain a good relationship with journalists, he will be most forthcoming to the people who have written positive stories about the client in the past.

Publicists handle all interview requests for a celebrity, politician, author or other public figure. To protect the client from any surprises, publicists will ask the journalist exactly what the story is about and what questions he plans to ask. In some cases, the publicist will ask to be present at the interview to make sure that the client doesn't comment on sensitive issues or make remarks that could look bad in the papers.

Publicists often organize press tours for actors, celebrities and authors. The publicist makes all the travel arrangements for the client, sets up locations, arranges for press passes and even accompanies the client on the road.

More than ever, publicists network with online bloggers and read and respond to comments on popular social networks. In addition to a standard press tour, they might arrange for a live, online Q&A session with a popular fan site or interviews with podcasts.

Required Skills to be a Publicist

The most important skill for a publicist is the ability to think like a journalist. Journalists and editors need publicists as much as publicists need them. Editors need to fill the pages of their newspapers, magazine and Web sites. They need stories tailored to their readers' interests. Celebrity and entertainment writers, in particular, rely on tips from publicists to keep their sections original and exciting.

This means that publicists need excellent communication skills both written and on the phone.

But a publicist does need other skills including being a natural "people person." He needs to be outgoing, funny and not afraid of rejection. The best publicists establish genuine relationships with the editors and reporters who cover their client. They know how to network without looking like they're networking. They earn the trust of journalists by always being honest and available for comment. They understand that a good idea from a good person will get much more attention than a lot of exclamation points from a used car salesman.

Patience and flexibility are extremely important for publicists as celebrities, politicians or other public figures can be difficult to work with. They hold odd hours, have bad habits and live in a media fishbowl. A publicist needs to be able to work within their client's time frame.

Like any career in public relations, publicists need to be able to deal with crises and emergencies with a calm head. They look for ways to turn mistakes into PR opportunities. When a rock star is busted for a DUI, the publicist needs to make sure there's a story in the next week's paper about the celebrity coming out of rehab and volunteering with Mothers Against Drunk Driving.

How do you break into the publicist business? Do you need a special college degree or can you just work your way up?

Becoming a Publicist

Strong written and oral communication skills are essential to becoming a publicist, so a lot of future publicists major in communications, journalism and public relations in college. That said, there's no specific college degree that guarantees success as a publicist. Good publicists are generally well read with a broad liberal arts education. Advanced degrees are not necessary.

To become a publicist, you need to start at the bottom, gain on-the-job experience and work your way up the ranks. A good place to start is with an internship while you're in college. Public relations firms, literary agencies and talent agencies are good places to look for publicity internships. Interns are expected to do some of the least glamorous work like pick up rental cars and dry cleaning for the client, run to Starbucks for the office staff and conduct online research.

With some internship experience, you could land an entry-level job as a publicist's assistant. In this capacity, you might answer phones, help the publicist draft press releases, keep the publicist's calendar, assemble press kits, research journalists and make arrangements for press tours. Assistants are expected to be on-call, sometimes at odd hours and always reachable through a cell phone or BlackBerry. As a perk, you may get to attend parties, hang out with famous people and share in some of the free gifts.

To move up from an assistant position, you need to start making contacts within the publicity industry and the media. Being an assistant is a great place to start, because you can piggyback on the network of contacts already in your boss's Rolodex. You need to show your boss and members of the media that you're reliable, a solid writer and that you have a nose for a good news story.

Even as an intern or an assistant, consider joining one of the established industry groups like the Public Relations Society of America or the National Council for Marketing and Public Relations. These groups hold conferences; workshops and information sessions that can help you network with fellow publicity professionals.

In the end, your success as a publicist will depend on how well you represent your clients. If you can get great press for a lesser-known client, then bigger-name celebrities will know that you can handle higher-profile, higher-maintenance clients. The nature of celebrity is fleeting, so expect some dry spells during any publicity career. One day you're representing Angelina Jolie, and the next day you're pitching stories for Hulk Hogan. The important thing is to get some sort of satisfaction and thrill from working with public figures and the media.

*****

Here are some of the publicists you should use:

http://www.nationalpublicist.com/
http://nissenpr.com/
http://www.payperclip.com
http://www.coopersmithagency.com/

I personally prefer using a publicist but don't go run out and hire one until you have gotten your feet wet and learned something about the business. This will help you evaluate and hire a good publicist that fits your needs and type of business you are in.

I specialize in book publishing and forensics science and I have separate publicists for each topic.

Getting freed publicity is not difficult but it does require that you develop a plan just like a business plan but for marketing and advertising purposes.

In this plan you want to outline your goals and it isn't enough to simply state "I want to sell my products/services." You need to articulate what sites and services you need to access to obtain your goals.

There is a wealth of information in this book and hundreds of websites to study carefully and put in your plan. Be sure to study the sties carefully. Many will not be what you are looking for but I have only listed the sites that I have used or I have experience with over my 32-year career as a publisher and investigator.

Every good thing has a bad side so in your plan outline the negatives and what to watch out for. Be careful of people asking for money upfront and check out online all companies and services that you are contemplating using.

For those of you that like to keep things simple, go here: http://publicityhound.com/.

Joan Stewart is a good all around publicist and knows her stuff so talk to her.

Okay, thanks for reading my book. Now I have a special gift for you…

I Have a Special Gift for My Readers

I appreciate my readers for without them I am just another author attempting to make a difference. If my book has made a favorable impression please leave me an honest review.   Thank you in advance for you participation.

My readers and I have in common a passion for the written word as well as the desire to learn and grow from books.

My special offer to you is a massive ebook library that I have compiled over the years. It contains hundreds of fiction and non-fiction ebooks in Adobe Acrobat PDF format as well as the Greek classics and old literary classics too.

In fact, this library is so massive to completely download the entire library will require over 5 GBs open on your desktop.

Use the link below and scan all of the ebooks in the library. You can select the ebooks you want individually or download the entire library.

The link below does not expire after a given time period so you are free to return for more books rather than clog your desktop. And feel free to give the link to your friends who enjoy reading too.

I thank you for reading my book and hope if you are pleased that you will leave me an honest review so that I can improve my work and or write books that appeal to your interests.

Okay, here is the link…

http://tinyurl.com/special-readers-promo

PS: If you wish to reach me personally for any reason you may simply write to mailto:support@epubwealth.com.

I answer all of my emails so rest assured I will respond.

Meet the Author

Dr. Leland Benton is Director of Applied Web Info, a holding company for ePubWealth.com, a leading ePublisher company based in Utah. With over 21,000 resellers in over 22-countries, ePubWealth.com is a leader in ePublishing, book promotion, and ebook marketing.

As the creator and author of "The ePubWealth Program," Leland teaches up-and-coming authors the ins-and-outs of today's ePublishing world. He has assisted hundreds of authors make it big in the ePublishing world.

Leland also created a series of external book promotion programs and teaches authors how to promote their books using external marketing sources.

Leland is also the Managing Director of Applied Mind Sciences, the company's mind research unit and Chief Forensics Investigator for the company's ForensicsNation unit. He is active in privacy rights through the company's PrivacyNations unit and is an expert in survival planning and disaster relief through the company's SurvivalNations unit.

Leland resides in Southern Utah.

Visit some of his websites
http://appliedmindsciences.com/
http://appliedwebinfo.com/
http://BoolbuilderPLUS.com
http://embarrassingproblemsfix.com/
http://www.epubwealth.com/
http://forensicsnation.com/
http://neternatives.com/
http://privacynations.com/
http://survivalnations.com/
http://thebentonkitchen.com
http://theolegions.org